Cookie Recipes

Hannie P. Scott

CONTENTS

ACKNOWLEDGMENTS

I am so grateful for those of you who make up the community of readers that I love to write recipe books for! Thank you for your shares, encouraging emails, feedback, and reviews. I appreciate each one more than you guys know.

Abbreviations

oz = ounce

fl oz = fluid ounce

tsp = teaspoon

tbsp = tablespoon

ml = milliliter

c = cup

pt = pint

qt = quart

gal = gallon

L = liter

Conversions

1/2 fl oz = 3 tsp = 1 tbsp = 15 ml

1 fl oz = 2 tbsp = 1/8 c = 30 ml

2 fl oz = 4 tbsp = 1/4 c = 60 ml

4 fl oz = 8 tbsp = 1/2 c = 118 ml

8 fl oz = 16 tbsp = 1 c = 236 ml

16 fl oz = 1 pt = 1/2 qt = 2 c = 473 ml

128 fl oz = 8 pt = 4 qt = 1 gal = 3.78 L

Chocolate Chip Cookies
Makes 14-18 cookies

What you need:

3/4 cup butter, softened
3/4 cup packed brown sugar
1/4 cup white sugar
1 egg
1 tsp vanilla extract
2 cups all-purpose flour

1 3.5-oz package instant vanilla pudding mix
1 tsp baking soda
A pinch of salt
2 cups chocolate chips

What to do:

1. Line a baking sheet with parchment paper.
2. In a large bowl, combine the butter, sugars, egg, and vanilla and beat with a mixer until creamed.
3. Slowly mix in the flour, pudding mix, baking soda, and salt and mix for about 1 minute.
4. Slowly mix in the chocolate chips.
5. Form the dough into 14-18 balls and place them on your prepared baking sheet.
6. Cover the baking sheet with plastic wrap and place it in the fridge for 2 hours or the freezer for 15 minutes.
7. Preheat your oven to 350 degrees F.
8. Bake the cookies for 11 minutes or until the edges are slightly golden. They will firm up more after you remove them from the oven.
9. Remove the cookies from the oven and let cool for 10 minutes before serving or storing in an airtight container.

Lemon Butter Cookies
Servings: 30

What you need:
1 cup butter, at room temperature
2/3 cup sugar
1 egg
2 tsp lemon zest
1 tbsp lemon juice
2 1/2 cups all-purpose flour

What to do:
1. Preheat your oven to 350 degrees F and line a baking sheet with parchment paper.
2. With an electric mixer, cream together the butter and sugar in a large bowl.
3. Beat in the egg, lemon zest, and lemon juice.
4. Gradually mix in the flour until mixed well.
5. Roll the dough into 1 inch balls and place on the prepared sheet.
6. Bake for 15 minutes or until the cookies are slightly golden on the bottom.
7. Remove from the oven and let cool on the baking sheet for a couple minutes then transfer to a wire cooling rack to cool completely before serving.

Chocolate Caramel Cookies
Makes 2 1/2 dozen

What you need:
1 package devil's food cake mix
2 eggs
1/2 cup canola oil
42 Rolo candies
M&M's

What to do:
1. Preheat your oven to 350 degrees F and line 2 baking sheets with parchment paper.
2. In a large bowl, mix together the cake mix, eggs, and oil.
3. Roll the dough into tbsp sized balls and place 1-2 inches apart on the prepared baking sheets.
4. Press a Rolo into each ball.
5. Bake for 8-10 minutes.
6. As soon as you remove the cookies from the oven, press 4 M&M's onto each cookie.
7. Let cool and serve!

Nutella Cookies
Makes 1 dozen

What you need:
1 roll of chocolate chip cookie dough, at room temperature
1 cup Nutella
3 tbsp unsweetened cocoa powder
3/4 tsp ground cinnamon
6 large marshmallows, cut in half

What to do:
1. Preheat your oven to 350 degrees and line two baking sheets with parchment paper.
2. In a large bowl, break up the cookie dough and add the Nutella, cocoa powder, and cinnamon.
3. Beat with an electric mixer until well mixed.
4. Shape the dough into 12 2-inch balls. Flatten the balls and place half of a large marshmallow in the center of each and fold the dough around the marshmallow.
5. Place the balls 2-inches apart on the baking sheets and bake for 10-12 minutes.
6. Cool on the pan for 5 minutes then transfer to a rack to cool completely before serving.

White Chocolate Cranberry Cookies
Makes about 2 dozen

What you need:

3/4 cup butter, at room temperature

3/4 cup brown sugar

1/4 cup granulated sugar

1 large egg, at room temperature

2 tbsp vanilla extract

2 cups all-purpose flour

2 tsp cornstarch

1 tsp baking soda

1/2 tsp salt

3/4 cup white chocolate chips

1/4 cup dried cranberries

What to do:

1. In a large mixing bowl, beat the butter, brown sugar, and granulated sugar with a mixer until smooth and creamy.
2. Add the egg and vanilla and mix together.
3. In a separate bowl, stir together the flour, cornstarch, baking soda, and salt.
4. Slowly mix the flour mixture into the wet mixture until well combined.
5. Stir in the white chocolate chips and dried cranberries.
6. Chill the dough for at least 2 hours.
7. Preheat your oven to 350 degrees F and line a large baking sheet or two with parchment paper.
8. Roll the dough into 1-inch balls and place on the baking sheet(s) 1-2 inches apart.
9. Bake for 8-10 minutes or until golden around the edges.
10. Allow the cookie to cool on the sheet for 5 minutes then transfer to a wire rack to cool.
11. Serve or store in an airtight container.

Red Velvet Cookies
Makes 2 dozen

What you need:
1 box red velvet cake mix
6 tbsp butter, melted
1 cup powdered sugar
1 tsp cornstarch
2 eggs

What to do:
1. Preheat your oven to 375 degrees F and line a baking sheet with parchment paper.
2. Combine the cornstarch and powdered sugar in a small bowl.
3. In a large bowl, combine the cake mix, melted butter, and eggs. Mix on low with an electric mixer.
4. Roll into 1-inch balls and roll in the powdered sugar/cornstarch mixture.
5. Place balls 2-inches apart on the prepared baking sheet.
6. Bake for 9-11 minutes or until set.
7. Let cool on the baking sheets for 5 minutes before transferring to a wire rack to cool completely.

Snicker Doodles

Makes 2 dozen

What you need:

1/2 cup shortening

3/4 cup granulated sugar

1 egg

1 tbsp vanilla

1 1/2 cups all-purpose flour

1/2 tsp baking soda

1/4 tsp cream of tartar

1 tbsp cinnamon

3 tbsp granulated sugar

What to do:

1. Preheat your oven to 350 degrees and line a baking sheet with parchment paper.
2. Cream together the shortening and sugar in a mixing bowl with an electric mixer.
3. Add the egg and vanilla and mix well.
4. In a separate bowl, combine the flour, baking soda, salt, and cream of tartar and mix well.
5. Slowly add the dry ingredients to the wet ingredients.
6. Roll the dough into 1 inch balls.
7. In a small bowl, mix together 1 tbsp of cinnamon and 3 tbsp of sugar.
8. Roll the dough balls into the cinnamon and sugar mixture.
9. Place the balls on the prepared baking sheet and bake for 9-11 minutes or until edges are golden.
10. Let cool on the baking sheet for 5 minutes before transferring to a wire rack to cool completely.

Sugar Cookies
Makes 40-50 cookies

What you need:

1 cup butter, at room temperature

1 1/4 cup sugar

1 egg

1 1/2 tsp vanilla extract

1/2 tsp almond extract

3 cups flour

1 1/2 tsp baking powder

1/4 tsp salt

Colored sugar, sprinkles, or icing-for decorating

What to do:
1. In a large mixing bowl, cream together the butter and sugar until fluffy.
2. Add in the egg, vanilla extract, and almond extract until well combined.
3. In another bowl, combine the flour, baking powder, and salt.
4. Slowly add the flour mixture to the sugar mixture and mix.
5. Roll the dough with a rolling pin between 2 sheets of parchment or wax paper and place on a baking sheet.
6. Refrigerate for 30 minutes.
7. Preheat your oven to 350 degrees F and line 2 baking sheets with parchment paper.
8. Cut the dough into shapes using cookie cutter and transfer to a baking sheet.
9. Sprinkle with colored sugars (if using) and bake for 8-12 minutes.
10. Cool on the baking sheet for 5 minutes then transfer to a rack to cool completely.
11. Store in an airtight container.

Peppermint Cookies
Makes about 3 dozen

What you need:
1 cup butter, at room temperature

1/2 cup powdered sugar

1/2 tsp peppermint extract

1 1/4 cup all-purpose flour

1/2 cup cornstarch

2 tbsp butter, softened

1 1/2 cups powdered sugar

2 tbsp milk

1/4 tsp peppermint extract

1/2 cup crushed soft peppermints

What to do:
1. Line 2 baking sheets with parchment paper and preheat your oven to 350 degrees F.
2. In a mixing bowl, cream together 1 cup of butter and 1/2 cup powdered sugar until fluffy.
3. Add in the peppermint extract.
4. In a separate bowl, mix together the flour and cornstarch and gradually add it to the butter/sugar mixture and mix well, making a dough.
5. Shape the dough into 1 inch balls. Place them 2 inches apart on the prepared baking sheets.
6. Bake for 10 minutes or until the bottoms are light brown.
7. Let the cookies cool on the baking sheets for 5 minutes then transfer to a wire rack to cool completely.
8. In a small bowl, beat 2 tbsp butter, 1 1/2 cups powdered sugar, 2 tbsp milk, and 1/4 tsp peppermint extract. Mix until smooth, making the icing.
9. Spread the icing over the cooled cookies and sprinkle with crushed peppermints.

M&M Cookies
Makes 2 1/2 dozen

What you need:

2 ½ cups all-purpose flour

2 tsp cornstarch

3/4 tsp baking powder

1/2 tsp baking soda

1 cup butter

1 cup brown sugar

1/2 cup white sugar

1 large egg

2 tsp vanilla extract

1 11-oz bag M&M's

What to do:

1. Preheat your oven to 375 degrees and line 2 baking sheets with parchment paper.
2. In a mixing bowl, whisk together the flour, cornstarch, baking powder, baking soda, and salt. Set aside.
3. In a separate mixing bowl, mix together the butter and sugar with an electric mixer until creamy.
4. Mix in the egg and the additional egg yolk.
5. Mix in the vanilla.
6. Slowly mix in the flour mixture until combined.
7. Stir in the M&M's with a spoon, reserve 1/4 cup of M&M's for the tops of the cookies.
8. Scoop out 2 tbsp of dough at a time and form into a balls then place on the prepared baking sheet 2 inches apart.
9. Bake for 10-12 minutes until the edges are golden.
10. Allow the cookies to cool on the baking sheet for 5 minutes then transfer to a wire rack to cool completely.

Butterfinger Cookies
Makes 2 1/2 dozen

What you need:
1 3/4 cups all-purpose flour
3/4 tsp baking soda
1/4 tsp salt
3/4 cup granulated sugar
1/2 cup butter, softened
1 large egg
8 fun sized Butterfingers, chopped

What to do:
1. Preheat your oven to 350 degrees F.
2. In a mixing bowl, combine the flour, baking soda, and salt. Set aside.
3. In a separate mixing bowl, beat the sugar and butter with an electric mixer until creamy then mix in the egg.
4. Slowly mix in the flour mixture.
5. Stir in the Butterfinger pieces with a spoon.
6. Drop tablespoonfuls of dough onto prepared baking sheet 2 inches apart.
7. Bake for 10-12 minutes or until lightly golden.
8. Allow the cookies to cool for 5 minutes then transfer them to a wire rack to cool completely.

Cake Batter Cookies
Makes 2 dozen

What you need:

1 1/4 cups all-purpose flour

1 1/4 cup yellow boxed cake mix

1/2 tsp baking soda

3/4 cup butter, softened

1/2 cup sugar

1/2 cup brown sugar

1 egg

1 1/2 tsp vanilla extract

1 cup white chocolate chips

1/2 cup multicolored sprinkles

What to do:

1. In a large bowl, sift together the flour, cake mix, and baking soda.
2. In another large bowl, mix together (with a hand mixer) the butter and both sugars until smooth.
3. Add in the egg and mix for 1 minute until combined. Scrape down the sides of the bowl as needed.
4. Add the vanilla and mix until combined.
5. Add the flour mixture a little bit at a time at low speed until all of it is mixed in well.
6. Mix in the chocolate chips and sprinkles on low speed.
7. Cover and refrigerate the dough for at least 2 hours.
8. Preheat your oven to 350 degrees F and line 2 large baking sheets with parchment paper.
9. Form the dough into balls about 1 and a half tbsp each. Make the balls taller than they are round to make thicker cookies.
10. Bake the cookies for 10 mins or until the edges are browned.
11. Allow the cookies to cool for 5 mins on the baking sheet for 5 minutes then transfer them to a wire rack to cool completely.

Fruit Pizzas

Serves: 10

What you need:

10 sugar cookies (store bought or homemade)

4 oz cream cheese

4 oz whipped cream, thawed

1 cup powdered sugar

5 strawberries, sliced

1 cup blueberries

3 kiwis, peeled and sliced

What to do:

1. In a microwave safe bowl, microwave cream cheese for 30 seconds. If it isn't super soft, microwave for a few more seconds.
2. Add whipped cream to softened cream cheese and mix with an electric mixer until smoothed together.
3. Mix in powdered sugar.
4. Spread cream cheese mixture onto cookies.
5. Place fruit on cookies. I usually put the blueberries on the edge in a circle then put a slice of strawberry and kiwi in the middle.

Oreo Peppermint Cookies
Makes 36 cookies

What you need:
1 box white cake mix
1 stick butter, melted
1 egg
1/2 tsp peppermint extract
1/2 tsp vanilla extract
4 oz cream cheese, softened and cubed
1 cup crushed Oreos
1 cup Andes Peppermint Crunch pieces
1/2 cup chocolate chips

What to do:
1. In a mixing bowl, combine the cake mix, melted butter, egg, peppermint extract, and vanilla extract. Beat until a dough forms.
2. Add the cream cheese to the dough and mix until combined.
3. Stir in the peppermint crunch pieces and chocolate chips.
4. Stir in the crushed Oreos gently.
5. Refrigerate the dough for 30 minutes.
6. Preheat your oven to 350 degrees F and line a baking sheet or two with parchment paper and spray with non-stick spray.
7. Roll the dough into balls and line them 1-inch apart on the prepared pans.
8. Bake for 9-10 minutes.
9. Remove the pans from the oven and let the cookies sit for 2 minutes before transferring to a wire rack or a sheet of wax paper to cool completely.

Oreo Cheesecake Cookies
Servings: 12

What you need:
4 oz cream cheese, softened
8 tbsp salted butter, softened
3/4 cup sugar
1 cup all-purpose flour
10 Oreos, broken into pieces

What to do:
1. Beat the cream cheese and butter until fluffy with a mixer in a large bowl.
2. Add in the sugar and mix well.
3. Add in the flour, a little bit at a time on low until combined.
4. Fold in the Oreos with a spoon.
5. Cover the bowl and refrigerate for 30 minutes or freeze for 10 minutes.
6. Preheat your oven to 350 degrees F and line a large baking sheet with parchment paper.
7. Drop 2 tbsp sized balls of dough onto the baking sheet.
8. Bake for 9-11 minutes or until barely golden at the edges.
9. Remove from the oven and cool for 5 minutes, then transfer them to a cooling rack to cool completely before serving.

Peanut Butter Cookies
Serves: 8-10

What you need:
1 1/4 cup all-purpose flour
1 tsp baking soda
1/2 tsp salt
1/2 cup peanut butter
1 stick butter, softened
3/4 cup packed brown sugar
1/4 cup granulated sugar
1 large egg
1 tsp vanilla extract

What to do:
1. Preheat your oven to 350 degrees F.
2. Line two baking sheets with parchment paper.
3. Combine the flour, baking soda and salt in a medium bowl and set aside.
4. In a separate bowl, beat the peanut butter, butter, brown sugar, and granulated sugar until fluffy.
5. Add in the egg and vanilla.
6. Gradually add in the flour mixture on low speed. Beat until dough forms.
7. Drop 1 tbsp rounded balls of cookie dough onto prepared cookie sheets, leaving an inch or more between each.
8. Bake for 12 minutes or until edges are slightly browned.
9. Remove from the oven. Make crisscross fork marks on the top of the cookies before letting them cool completely. Serve or store in airtight container.

Peanut Butter and Nutella Cookies
Serves: 6-10

What you need:
1 cup butter
1 cup peanut butter
1 cup sugar
1 cup brown sugar
2 eggs
2 tsp vanilla
2 2/3 cup flour
2 tsp baking soda
1 tsp salt
1/2 cup Nutella

What to do:
1. Preheat your oven to 350 degrees F.
2. Cream butter, peanut butter, sugar, brown sugar, eggs, and vanilla together in large mixing bowl with mixer until smooth.
3. Combine the flour, salt, and baking soda in a separate bowl.
4. Add flour mixture to butter mixture slowly.
5. Add drops of Nutella over the dough and stir in gently.
6. Refrigerate the dough for 20 minutes to firm it up nicely.
7. Spoon dough onto greased baking sheet.
8. Bake for 8-10 minutes, or until slightly brown at edges.

Chocolate Caramel Cookies
Makes 2 1/2 dozen

What you need:
1 package devil's food cake mix
2 eggs
1/2 cup canola oil
42 Rolo candies
M&M's

What to do:
1. Preheat your oven to 350 degrees F and line 2 baking sheets with parchment paper.
2. In a large bowl, mix together the cake mix, eggs, and oil.
3. Roll the dough into tbsp sized balls and place 1-2 inches apart on the prepared baking sheets.
4. Press a Rolo into each ball.
5. Bake for 8-10 minutes.
6. As soon as you remove the cookies from the oven, press 4 M&M's onto each cookie.
7. Let cool and serve!

Gingerbread Cookies
Makes 24 cookies

What you need:

1/2 cup butter, softened

1/2 cup butter flavored shortening

1 1/2 cups sugar

1 egg

1 tbsp vanilla

3 tbsp molasses

3 cups all-purpose flour

2 tbsp baking soda

2 tsp ground cinnamon

1 tsp ground ginger

1/2 tsp ground cloves

1/2 tsp salt

Frosting

What to do:

1. In a large mixing bowl, cream together the butter, shortening, and sugar. Add in the egg, vanilla and molasses and mix well.
2. In a separate bowl, whisk together the flour, baking soda, cinnamon, ginger, ground cloves, and salt.
3. Add the flour mixture to the butter mixture a little bit at a time until it is all mixed in well. It will be thick!
4. Cover and refrigerate the dough for at least 2 hours.
5. Preheat your oven to 375 degrees F.
6. Lightly flour a large cutting board or sheet of wax paper.
7. Roll the dough on the floured surface and roll out into a sheet 1/4 inch thick.
8. Using a gingerbread man (or whatever shape you want!) cookie cutter, cut the dough.
9. Place the cut dough onto a greased baking sheet.
10. Bake for 10-12 minutes.
11. Let the cookies cool then decorate them with frosting.

Chocolate Peppermint Cookies

Servings: 15

What you need:

3/4 cup butter, softened

1/2 cup brown sugar, packed

1/2 cup sugar

1 egg

1/2 tsp vanilla extract

1/2 tsp peppermint extract

1 1/4 cups all-purpose flour

1/2 cup cocoa

1 tsp baking soda

1/2 cup Andes Peppermint Crunch pieces

3/4 cup chopped Oreos

What to do:

1. In a mixing bowl, cream together the butter and sugar until light and fluffy.
2. Mix in the egg and vanilla extract.
3. In a separate bowl, whisk together the flour, cocoa, and baking powder until combined.
4. Gradually add the flour mixture to the butter and sugar mixture and mix until combined well.
5. Cover and refrigerate for at least an hour.
6. Preheat your oven to 350 degrees F and line a baking sheet with parchment paper.
7. Form the dough into 1-2 inch balls and place them on the baking sheet 1-inch apart.
8. Bake for 8-10 minutes or until the edges look firm. The middle should still look soft.
9. Remove from the oven and cool for 2 minutes before transferring to a wire rack to cool completely.

ABOUT THE AUTHOR

Hannie's vision is to write a series of recipe books, each focusing on one theme or one type of food that could can be EASILY prepared by someone who wouldn't be considered your typical cook. She urges her readers to feel welcome to share recipes, thoughts, and ideas with her and any feedback is encouraged.

For more recipe books visit hanniepscott.com

Printed in Great Britain
by Amazon